WHAT IS GROUNDHOG DAY?

BY MAXIMILIAN SMITH

Gareth Stevens
PUBLISHING

Please visit our website, www.garethstevens.com. For a free color catalog of all our high-quality books, call toll free 1-800-542-2595 or fax 1-877-542-2596.

Library of Congress Cataloging-in-Publication Data

Smith, Maximilian.
 What is Groundhog Day? / Maximilian Smith.
    pages cm. — (The history of our holidays)
 Includes bibliographical references and index.
ISBN 978-1-4824-3832-1 (pbk.)
ISBN 978-1-4824-3833-8 (6 pack)
ISBN 978-1-4824-3834-5 (library binding)
1. Groundhog Day—Juvenile literature. I. Title.
 GT4995.G76S65 2016
 394.261—dc23

                                     2015018174

Published in 2016 by
Gareth Stevens Publishing
111 East 14th Street, Suite 349
New York, NY 10003

Designer: Sarah Liddell
Editor: Therese Shea

Photo credits: Cover, p. 1 Alex Wong/Staff/Getty Images News/Getty Images;
p. 5 Archie Carpenter/Stringer/Getty Images News/Getty Images;
p. 7 (badger) Dennis W. Donohue/Shutterstock.com; p. 7 (bear) Eduard Kyslynskyy/
Shutterstock.com; p. 9 De Agostini Picture Library/De Agostini/Getty Images;
p. 11 AFP/Stringer/AFP/Getty Images; pp. 13, 15, 17, 19 Jeff Swensen/Stringer/
Getty Images News/Getty Images; p. 21 Shahar Azran/Contributor/WireImage/
Getty Images.

Printed in the United States of America

CPSIA compliance information: Batch #CW16GS: For further information contact Gareth Stevens, New York, New York at 1-800-542-2595.

CONTENTS

Boldface words appear in the glossary.

Happy Groundhog Day!

Each winter, many people gather in a small town in Pennsylvania. They wait for a groundhog that lives near there to appear. He's said to be able to **forecast** when spring will come. It's February 2—Groundhog Day!

Forecasting Spring

Hundreds of years ago, people began to believe that animals could forecast the weather. They thought that animals that **hibernated** through the winter, such as bears and badgers, came out of their **burrows** on February 2.

badger

bear

If it was a sunny day, the animal saw its **shadow** and would go back into its burrow. The shadow meant there would be 6 more weeks of winter weather. So, the animal would begin to hibernate again.

9

If it was a cloudy day, the animal wouldn't see its shadow. It would stop hibernating and get ready for spring. The animal knew that warm weather was coming. At least, that's what people believed!

Punxsutawney Phil

When Germans moved to Pennsylvania, they brought these beliefs with them. They thought groundhogs there could forecast the coming spring. Since 1887, the town of Punxsutawney, Pennsylvania, has had the most famous weather-forecasting groundhog: Punxsutawney Phil.

Punxsutawney
Phil

13

Each year, TV and newspaper reporters and thousands more travel to Pennsylvania to learn what Punxsutawney Phil **predicts** on February 2. He comes out of his burrow in Gobbler's Knob and is said to tell his forecast to the Groundhog Club President.

SHOW US YOUR SHADOW

Is Punxsutawney Phil always right about the coming weather? The Inner Circle, the people who care for him throughout the year, say he is. However, other records say he's right less than half the time.

Groundhogs only live 6 to 8 years. So, how has Phil been forecasting since 1887? Phil's caretakers say they give him a magic drink each summer to make him live longer! More likely, there have been many Phils over the years.

More Forecasters

Canada has a groundhog that forecasts the weather called Wiarton Willie. New York has Staten Island Chuck, and North Carolina has Sir Walter Wally. There are other groundhogs said to predict spring, too. Is there one near you? Happy Groundhog Day!

Staten Island
Chuck

S.I. CHUCK SAYS
ZOO
Staten Island Zoo

Spring
is
Coming

GLOSSARY

burrow: a hole made by an animal in which it lives or hides

forecast: to guess something will happen

hibernate: to be in a sleeplike state for an extended period of time, usually during winter

predict: to guess what will happen in the future based on facts or knowledge

shadow: a dark shape on a surface that falls behind someone or something blocking light

FOR MORE INFORMATION

BOOKS

Herrington, Lisa M. *Groundhog Day*. New York, NY: Children's Press, 2014.

Murray, Julie. *Groundhog Day*. Minneapolis, MN: ABDO Publishing Company, 2014.

Peppas, Lynn. *Groundhog Day*. New York, NY: Crabtree Publishing, 2010.

WEBSITES

Groundhog
animals.nationalgeographic.com/animals/mammals/groundhog/
Find out much more about the animal called the groundhog.

Groundhog Day
www.groundhog.org
Read about Groundhog Day in Punxsutawney, Pennsylvania, on this site.

INDEX